T0329424

CAMBRIDGE LIBRARY COLLECTION

Books of enduring scholarly value

Cambridge

The city of Cambridge received its royal charter in 1201, having already been home to Britons, Romans and Anglo-Saxons for many centuries. Cambridge University was founded soon afterwards and celebrates its octocentenary in 2009. This series explores the history and influence of Cambridge as a centre of science, learning, and discovery, its contributions to national and global politics and culture, and its inevitable controversies and scandals.

The Story of Cambridgeshire

William Cunningham (1849–1919) was one of the most eminent economic historians of his generation. The author of The Growth of English Industry and Commerce (1882) is seen in a different role in this very approachable and informative set of talks. Early in his career, Cunningham worked as an extension lecturer, and in these six lectures given to teachers on aspects of local history he displays great flair in communicating how history can be brought to life in the classroom. From the creation of the fen landscape in prehistoric times to the historic buildings of its towns, Cunningham explains the unique position and history of Cambridgeshire as a county distinct from its neighbours. He shows teachers how to inspire an interest in history in their pupils by engaging with the parts they can recognise: the surviving buildings, landscapes and traditions of their county, an approach still successful in schools today.

Cambridge University Press has long been a pioneer in the reissuing of out-of-print titles from its own backlist, producing digital reprints of books that are still sought after by scholars and students but could not be reprinted economically using traditional technology. The Cambridge Library Collection extends this activity to a wider range of books which are still of importance to researchers and professionals, either for the source material they contain, or as landmarks in the history of their academic discipline.

Drawing from the world-renowned collections in the Cambridge University Library, and guided by the advice of experts in each subject area, Cambridge University Press is using state-of-the-art scanning machines in its own Printing House to capture the content of each book selected for inclusion. The files are processed to give a consistently clear, crisp image, and the books finished to the high quality standard for which the Press is recognised around the world. The latest print-on-demand technology ensures that the books will remain available indefinitely, and that orders for single or multiple copies can quickly be supplied.

The Cambridge Library Collection will bring back to life books of enduring scholarly value across a wide range of disciplines in the humanities and social sciences and in science and technology.

The Story of Cambridgeshire

CUNNINGHAM

CAMBRIDGE UNIVERSITY PRESS

Cambridge New York Melbourne Madrid Cape Town Singapore São Paolo Delhi

Published in the United States of America by Cambridge University Press, New York

www.cambridge.org
Information on this title: www.cambridge.org/9781108003414

This edition first published 1920
This digitally printed version 2009

ISBN 978-1-108-00341-4

THE
STORY OF CAMBRIDGESHIRE

CAMBRIDGE UNIVERSITY PRESS
C. F. CLAY, Manager
LONDON : FETTER LANE, E.C. 4

NEW YORK: THE MACMILLAN CO.
BOMBAY ⎫
CALCUTTA ⎬ MACMILLAN AND CO., Ltd.
MADRAS ⎭
TORONTO: THE MACMILLAN CO.
OF CANADA, Ltd.
TOKYO : MARUZEN-KABUSHIKI-KAISHA

THE STORY OF CAMBRIDGESHIRE

AS TOLD BY ITSELF

BEING SIX LECTURES
GIVEN TO TEACHERS

BY

W. CUNNINGHAM, D.D., F.B.A.

CAMBRIDGE
AT THE UNIVERSITY PRESS
1920

PRINTED IN GREAT BRITAIN BY
RICHARD CLAY & SONS, LIMITED,
BRUNSWICK ST., STAMFORD ST., S.E. 1,
AND BUNGAY. SUFFOLK.

CONTENTS

THE STORY OF
CAMBRIDGESHIRE

I

PREHISTORIC TIMES—THE FENS

WHEN Mr. Austin Keen was kind enough to invite me to give this course of lectures, I felt some hesitation about complying. For, as I know little of school work, and the difficulties you have to face, I was very doubtful whether I could say anything that would be a practical help to you. It occurred to me, however, that the work of all teachers is so far similar that, if I simply tried to draw on my own experience, you might perhaps find something for yourselves that seemed likely to be of service.

The chief difficulty I have found in teaching in the University has been to awaken the interest of my class. If they are interested, they will be very attentive, and be ready to take in what is said ; and if they are not interested, the whole work drags and becomes wearisome alike to teacher and taught. And it was my experience that very few people are much interested in the history of the past : they live in the present, and are inclined to let bygones be bygones and leave them alone. The stories we hear of people long ago are apt to make us feel that they were rather ignorant and very queer, and quite unlike ourselves in every way. But I have observed that the interest of students is roused when they recognise that, in spite of all the differences, the people long ago were very like ourselves, and when they begin to find links that connect them with ourselves.

The most obvious link of connection is given by places; each of the Cambridge colleges recalls, once a year, the names of the men who, centuries ago, provided the buildings and possessions which the fellows and scholars of that college enjoy to-day. There is a very real link between the present and the past in each college; and I found that many students were ready to take an interest in the bygone days of the place where they lived themselves, and in the doings of the people who used to live there long ago.

It is from this point of view that I wish to speak a little about Cambridgeshire; it is an interesting part of the country, because it is closely connected with many things of which we read in books. This is true, more or less, of every part of England, and makes it much more interesting to travel here than in some other countries. In new countries you may find a great deal that is wonderful and beautiful: the Falls of Niagara, and the Golden Gate at San Francisco; but there seem to be many places that have no associations with the past; they may have great

2

expectations, but they have not the special charm which comes from old associations. Cambridgeshire, however, is associated with much of what we read: with the struggles of S. Edmund and the victory of the Danes at Bartlow, with the final efforts of William of Normandy to conquer the Isle of Ely. We have all heard of Henry VII's great financier, Morton, who invented the dilemma known as Morton's Fork; but he becomes more interesting to us when we think of him as a man who found time, among all the cares of State, to try to improve the harbour at Wisbech, and to dig the channel, called Morton's Leam, between Peterborough and Wisbech. He was the great engineer who first took in hand the draining of the Fen systematically, and Vermüyden and the Duke of Bedford adopted his schemes and followed out his plans. Then we can get ample detail about Queen Elizabeth and her royal progresses, when we read of her visit here and the entertainment she received; or of Charles I as a prisoner at Childerley, or of Cromwell's camp on Triplow Heath. There are numberless associations with political events in the past which give a romantic interest to things and places that are familiar, and keep them from being commonplace.

We may go a little further. However great the interest may be of local associations with events of which we read, there is still greater interest in *trying to make out what features tell us themselves.* Such marked features as the Devil's Dyke at Newmarket and the Fleam Dyke at Fulbourn are prehistoric; we have no historical records about them, and they have no historical *association*, but they tell us something about themselves, and if we have skill to spell out what they mean, we learn a good deal. They are enormous earthworks, and they seem to have been made by the people in the Eastern Counties to defend themselves against raids from the southern Midlands. There is reason to believe that they were made before the Romans invaded Britain, and they are works which imply a great organisation of labour. If the men had only very simple tools, such as the horns of animals, to dig in the chalk, and baskets to carry the earth from the bottom of the ditch to the top of the dyke, the task would take a long time, and this seems likely enough; there must have been the means of feeding a multitude of labourers for many months. When we begin to think about these great undertakings, we see that the monuments which remain themselves tell us something about the men who made them.

There is great difficulty in spelling out these remains so as to read them aright; there has been much hasty guessing at the meaning of archæological remains, which has been discredited by later and careful research. There is most danger of going far wrong when we have no histories to help us, as is the case with prehistoric remains; but when we can take historical records and local remains together, and fit them in with one another, we find that they supplement one another. The historical record is sometimes very bald and bare, and yet becomes instinct with life when we can supplement it by what relics and remains tell us about the people who lived and worked in bygone times.

History becomes more interesting the more we realise that the men and women of whom we read were real people, and very like ourselves; and we get this impression most vividly when we pay attention to the evidence of what they did. As long as we only think of them as people in a book, and talk about them, they seem unreal, like any one else in a story-book or a fairy tale, but when we pay attention to what they *did* and what they left behind them, we feel that they were not merely in a story-book, but that they have a connection with ourselves and our own lives. And so it seems to me worth while to put the story of the past and the relics of the past together; the relics help to clothe the dry bones of names and dates, and to make them more vivid; and I shall try to call your attention to some of the illustrations we find ready to hand in Cambridgeshire.

To give a single instance of what I mean. We all know that William the Conqueror won a great victory at Hastings, and that, as Harold was killed, there was no one to rally the defeated troops or to organise general resistance. The country lay before William undefended; but he did not find it at all easy to establish his royal authority everywhere; there was local resistance here and there, and in no place was the resistance more protracted than in the Isle of Ely, where Hereward continued to defy the Conqueror. William had to make Cambridge the base of his operations against the " last of the English," to quote Kingley's phrase; and he erected a castle. There was no stone to be got close by, but he made a great mound of earth on the slope of the hill, and on the top he put a wooden "block-house," as we learned to call them in the South African War, from which he could survey the country that lay between him and Ely. He had to clear away houses in the town[1] to find what he thought a suitable site for his castle, and the ground on which it stands came directly under the authority of himself and his officials; the Castle Hill and the buildings on it are still outside the borough, and not under the jurisdiction of the Mayor, but of the County. The whole story of William's army of occupation and of his efforts to establish his authority becomes more vivid to me when I go up the Castle Hill, and trace the parts of the old town which he cleared away, and look across the open country to the great church at Ely, as he did from his wooden block-house.

The view, of course, is very different from what he saw : the distant Abbey buildings in his time were insignificant; to-day there is a wide stretch of cultivated land, whereas in his time very little of the land was under cultivation, and there were great stretches of marsh and waste. And this leads me to another point which I wish to make in this introductory lecture. The *people* in the past were more like the people we know than we are ready to think, but the *things*, and the conditions in which they lived,

[1] Domesday Book, I.

were extraordinarily different from those with which
we are familiar. Much of the soil of the great level
of the Fens is very rich, but it is liable to be flooded
by the rivers which come from the Midlands or from
Suffolk; and for centuries there has been a struggle
to keep it free from water; and even now there is
occasional trouble, if vigilance is relaxed, as was
recently the case at Suthery. The final efforts at
controlling these floods were made by a Dutchman
named Vermüyden, whose house, with a Dutch
inscription, can be seen at Fen Drayton; they are
well marked in the map of Cambridgeshire by the
Bedford rivers which carry the water of the Ouse
from Earith to Denver. But the Fens have a long
history, before the attempts to free them from flood.
In Roman times the danger was not from the rivers,
but from the sea, and the great level of the Fens
consisted of salt marshes like those on the Essex coast.
The Romans set themselves to reclaim these marshes
from the sea by raising a great *Vallum*, or bank, which
runs, by Walton and Walsoken and Walpole, from
Wisbech to Lynn. They were successful in keeping
out the sea, but their great engineering work had,
incidentally, another result that they had not fore-
seen. The channel at Wisbech began to silt up, so
that the water from the Midlands could not get out
to the sea, but began to make a new way for itself
to Lynn, and the flooding of the Fens with river water
began to be serious. There were local efforts to deal
with the evil here and there, like the grand banks at
Over, but even if these were not designed with the

7

deliberate intention of keeping the floods away from Over, and turning them on to Swavesey instead, they were mere palliatives, and it was not till Bishop Morton took the matter in hand that attempts to reclaim the drowned lands were systematically made, and that men recognised that spasmodic efforts in one parish or another were useless. There were great differences between what the Fens were in the Conqueror's time and what they are in ours.

The map was entirely different, because the Ouse and the Cam did not go into the sea at Lynn; they doubled back at Upware and Cottenham and Earith, and flowed into the sea at Wisbech, before the outlet there silted up. After the next lecture I shall be better able to explain the arguments which have convinced me that in the thirteenth century the course of the Ouse and Cam was deliberately altered, so as to flow past Ely, and to make an improved channel for traffic between Huntingdonshire and the seaport of Lynn.

But although the Fens were uncultivated in William the Conqueror's time, we must not think of them as quite useless and unproductive. Thomas of Ely enumerates the rich resources of the Fens, and shows that William would have had great difficulty in starving out the heroic little garrison there. A Norman knight who had lived in the Isle as a prisoner gives this account to William of the way in which he fared. "I tell you, sire, I have seen wild-fowl alone in that island enough to feed them all the year round. I was there in the moulting time, and saw them take—

8

one day one hundred, one two hundred; and once, as I am a belted knight, a thousand duck out of one single mere. There is a wood there, with herons sprawling about the tree-tops—I did not think there were so many in the world; otters and weasels, ermines and pole-cats, for fur robes; and fish for Lent and Fridays in every puddle and leat—pike and perch, roach and eels, on every old wife's table; while the knights think scorn of anything worse than smelt and burbot. . . . The island is half of it a garden— richer land, they say, is none in these realms, and I believe it : but, besides that, there is a deer-park there with a thousand head in it, red and fallow, beside hares; and plenty of swine and goats in woods, and sheep, and cattle : and if they fail there are plenty more to be got, they know where. . . . Out of every little island in their fens, for forty miles on end. There are the herds fattening themselves on the richest pastures in the land, and no man needing to herd them, for they are all safe among dykes and meres." [1]

The fens no longer abound with the resources which were plentiful nine hundred years ago; and we have interesting evidence as to the climate, which shows us how recent these changes have been. Defoe was a shrewd observer, and in making the tour of England, he rode along the high road from the Gogs to Cambridge. He writes : " As we descended West- ward, we saw the *Fenn* Country on our Right, almost all cover'd with Water, like a Sea, the *Michaelmas* Rains,

[1] Kingsley, *Hereward the Wake*, II. 126.

having been very great that Year, they had sent down great Floods of Water from the Upland Countries, and these Fenns being, as may be very properly said, the Sink of no less than thirteen Counties . . . they are often thus overflow'd. . . . As these Fenns appear cover'd with Water, so I observ'd too, that they generally at this latter part of the Year appear also cover'd with Foggs, so that when the Downs and higher Grounds of the adjacent Country were gilded with the Beams of the Sun, the Isle of *Ely* look'd wrapp'd up in Blankets, and nothing to be seen but now and then, the Lanthorn Cupola of Ely *Minster*.

" One could hardly see this from the Hills and not pity the many thousands of Families that were bound to or confin'd in those Foggs, and had no other Breath to draw than what must be mix'd with those Vapours, and that Steam which so universally overspread the Country : But notwithstanding this, the People, especially those that are used to it, live . . . as Healthy as other Folks, except now and then an Ague, which they make light of, and there are great Numbers of very antient People among them." [1]

The ague appears to be entirely a thing of the past, and March, which lies in the very centre of the Fens, seems to be very free from fog, and to enjoy its place in the sun.

[1] Defoe, *Tour* (1724), I. 119. Richardson reprints this passage as if it was still applicable in 1742.

II

THE IMMIGRANTS

THERE were two great waves of immigration which swept over the south of Great Britain between the Christian Era and the Norman Conquest; and though they differed from each other in every other way, they were alike in this, that both of them left their mark very deeply upon the face of the country.

The Romans were bent on systematic colonisation, and on bringing this island within the circle of the Roman Empire, so that they could draw on its resources for supplies of food, and for recruiting their armies. The tribes of Jutes and Saxons and Angles, and their cousins, the Danes, settled piecemeal, here and there, according as they were attracted by one district or another and as the fortune of war turned them; the Romans introduced a high civilisation from Southern lands, while the heathen tribes seemed to hold nothing sacred and were ruthless in the destruction they wrought.

The Romans proceeded systematically, both in planting the towns and in laying out the fields round each centre. Cambridge, on the other side of the river, is a very good example of the sort of town they laid out. Lincoln and Winchester are very similar; all

[1] Tacitus.

three lie on rising ground with a river at the foot, just outside the town. All three are oblong; and Cambridge was protected by a ditch and dyke of which we see remains in Mount Pleasant and in Chesterton Lane. At Lincoln the old Roman gateway is still preserved on the north side of the town. From each of the sides of the oblong four main roads went out, and, as we read, the blocks of land were plotted out along these roads in square holdings,[1] so that the country must have looked like the chessboard country in *Alice Through the Looking-Glass*. The work of the surveyors in laying out the land has been obliterated by successive generations who used the country according to their own requirements, and not as the Roman surveyors had intended, but many of the roads remain. In particular, we have the Huntingdon Road, which stretches out interminably towards the North, and the lines of other Roman roads in the county can be easily distinguished.

We are not rich in Roman remains in Cambridgeshire; but the coins and altars and pottery which have been found make it clear that the Romans lived and worked here habitually, and moulded the country to their model; but we could not get together a great collection of Roman remains, such as there is at Colchester or York, or show impressive Roman pieces of decoration such as those which remain at Leicester; but the Roman roads tell us about the essential thing in the Roman colonisation of this island. The Roman Empire was held together, as it were, by the roads;

[1] Coote, *The Romans of Britain.*

all roads led to Rome, and it was from Rome, as a centre, that all the vast area was controlled and governed. The roads gave the means of exerting military power, and of enforcing law and order.

There are many of our common things which the Romans introduced among us, such as apples, and quickset hedges; and Gregory the Great was not only full of missionary enterprise, but was also a great farmer, and encouraged the monks who settled here to improve the breeds of sheep and cattle. It is most impressive to stand at the great wall, which Hadrian built to mark the boundary of the Empire on the north and to defend it from the hostile tribes who had not been subdued; but from that northern boundary there were lines of communication which brought each part into direct connection with the distant centre, and each part was ruled and directed, not for its own independent life, but as a part of the whole.

Besides the roads the Romans laid out, there were other great public works which they carried through and which we are apt to overlook, because, since railways have come in, we have lost the sense of the importance of waterways for heavy traffic. Even I remember the time when the farmers at Horningsea sent their corn to market by barges, and Cambridge was long dependent on the river for its fuel and coals. The Romans developed a great system of water communication, which ramified through the county and gave extraordinary facilities for traffic; especially if, as seems likely, the Cam had a bigger body of water than to-day and barges could go farther. There are four columns in Ickleton Church which are each in one piece—a great block of stone : they are Barnack stone, and must have been brought from Northamptonshire. They very likely were originally meant to be the pediment of a Roman temple at Chesterford; but they stand now in Ickleton Church, and they must have been conveyed this long distance from the quarry. It seems to me most likely that they were brought by river, and they may help us to realise how much the Romans did for the water communication which was of extraordinary importance, all through the Middle Ages and till modern times, for heavy traffic. The roads were chiefly used for packhorses, and not for carts; and so districts which were served by water and had easy access to the sea had great advantages for trade. The Romans seem to have made a great canal, the Cair Dyke, which linked the Fen rivers, the Ouse and the Cam, with the Nene, and ran north from Peterborough to Lincoln, so as to make an internal waterway between our corn-growing region here in Cambridgeshire and the great centres of Roman administration at Lincoln and York.

This very hasty survey of the vestiges of the Roman occupation in Cambridgeshire, and the testimony they afford of systematic colonisation, may enable us to appreciate the extraordinary contrast in the long-timed and spasmodic raids of the heathen tribes who eventually settled in the country. There is a great deal of interesting detail in separating these tribes, and noting the distinctions we can trace between them : some of them had the habit of settling in villages, as was done in Cambridgeshire, while scattered hamlets, or even isolated houses, prevailed where the Celtic influence remained dominant. But from the time of Hengist and Horsa till the time of Canute, these tribes came as raiders, and were heathen, and only settled down gradually when they found a suitable district which they could wrest from their neighbours. There was nothing systematic about the immigration of these settlers, and there are no great public works to be ascribed to them. They could not continue to burn and plunder indefinitely, and when they determined to settle down themselves, they did not aim at introducing a civilisation or developing the country, but only at living for themselves, and we find a good deal of information in Cambridgeshire as to the manner in which those who settled here intended to live.

A map of Cambridgeshire which marks the separate parishes gives us the best idea of the groups which the original settlers formed, and the land which each group occupied. The parish, as an ecclesiastical term, is much later than some of the settlements which were undoubtedly made by tribes which were not Christian, and it seems to have begun with the desire to provide places for Christian burial in each locality; but the parish is our best representative of the original settlements of the English tribes.

When we look at the parish map of Cambridgeshire we are struck by the fact that the new settlers used the roads and rivers, which had been thoroughfares

15

for traffic among the Romans, as boundaries. They avoided the towns at first, and had little intercourse with their neighbours, so that they had no need to use the roads as the Romans did. But they found a new use for them as well-marked boundaries. They were people who greatly depended on their cattle, and good boundaries which marked the land of one village from another were essential to them, and they found these boundaries in the old roads. The Huntingdon Road is, for a great part of its course, a boundary between the villages which lie on each side of it, not a thoroughfare which connects them. It marks the line between Dry Drayton and Oakington and Long Stanton, between Lolworth and Boxworth and Swavesey, and between Conington and Dry Drayton. Then the old Roman road is the boundary between Cherry Hinton and Trumpington, between Fulbourn and Stapleford and Babraham, between Balsham and West Wickham on one side, and Abingdon, Hildersham, Linton and Horseheath on the other. The Ermine Street, from Royston to Godmanchester, was another great boundary line, which marks the division between Kneesworth and Bassingbourn, between Whaddon and Wendy, between Arrington and Wimpole, between Long Stowe and Bourne. There were older roads, which seem to have been important routes before the Romans came here and made their roads, such as the Icknield Way and the Mere Way, which also served as boundaries for the English settlements. It all makes us feel that the first settlers had no use for roads and means of communication, but lived off them altogether, and only used them to mark the confines of territory beyond which their cattle should not stray.

They turned the Roman waterways, too, to the same purpose. Of course, it was important that the cattle of each village should have access to water from which they could drink, but it is remarkable to notice how constantly the brooks and rivulets were used as marking the boundaries between settlements. I will only remind you how the main stream of the Cam separates Waterbeach from the Swaffhams and Horningsea, between Trumpington and Grantchester, between Great Shelford and Little Shelford and Hauxton, and then between Sawston, Pampisford and Hinxton on one side, and Whittlesford, Duxford and Ickleton on the other. The same sort of thing can be seen in regard to the other branches of the Cam and the Bourne Brook, but enough has been said to make us feel that it was very important to the settlers to have well-marked boundaries, so that they might keep their cattle from straying, for their main wealth was in their cattle. It may be that they were chiefly a pastoral people, and that cattle-rearing and milch-kine were their chief means of subsistence, a practice which remained true of Cottenham and Willingham and Soham till comparatively lately; but, at any rate, we shall be right in saying that pasture-farming was an essential part of the village economy and that the villages had little traffic with their neighbours.

THE STORY OF CAMBRIDGESHIRE

When we try to picture how the people of Cambridgeshire lived, not at the time when they first settled here, but just before the Norman Conquest, we find that they had added to their old mode of life or changed their habits so much that they were mainly given to the tillages, and that the cultivation of the soil was the most important of the village resources. We learn this from Domesday Book—the extraordinarily detailed account of the resources of his new kingdom which William had compiled as soon as he had really established his authority. It gives an enumeration of the arable area, and of the labour and the available stock in every village, and it is especially careful to show how far the land had suffered during the disturbances caused by the Norman Conquest. It has many retrospective references, and tells us about the normal condition of each village and of any special disability which made it temporarily poorer. The impression which the survey gives, is that of a people who were engaged in tillage as their chief means of sustenance.

There are relics of this primitive tillage, which remain here and there, and help to illustrate the mere enumerations which are recorded in the Survey. The agricultural practice was primitive : the settlers laid out the land best suited to tillage, but they would have found it extravagant not to use their arable fields, when the harvest was over, for grazing : they tried to keep as large a head of cattle and sheep as they could, so as to manure their fields; these were regularly cropped, and the crops were fenced off only by temporary fences which could be easily removed. There were, however, permanent balks which divided one strip in the fields from another, so that the land was permanently allotted; and each man's farm consisted of a number of strips which did not lie contiguously, but allowed each man to have a share of the good land as well as of the poorer soil. The balks which thus separated one strip of arable land from another remained untouched year by year, and were not ploughed up with the rest of the field, and here and there these balks remain still. They are very plainly visible on each side of the railway between Ashwell and Baldock, just outside the county at Cothall; and also between Triplow and Heydon; they may also be seen at Madingley, but they serve no useful purpose now and were recently ploughed up at Hildersham. But, wherever we come upon them, they are relics of the primitive tillage which the settlers in Cambridgeshire practised when they took to arable farming. The best way of solving the perennial problem of agriculture which the experience of the Middle Ages attained was that known as the three-field system, which gave the best opportunities for working the land and for maintaining the stock necessary to carry on the co-operative tillage.

There are other vestiges of the agriculture recorded in the Survey which remain in our day. The Domesday Survey enumerates a great number of mills; those could not be windmills, for the first known English windmill was built on the land of the Abbey of Bury in 1191.[1] They may have been horse-mills, and horses would be needed in connection with the mills to fetch the corn and carry back the flour, even where the horses did not supply the motive power. But the mills of which we read in the Domesday Survey are mostly along the line of the river or streams, and, as a fall of water was needed, they were probably at the points where mills are running now. There was a mill at Duxford, though it needed repair; there were mills at Thetford, Hauxton, Trumpington, Cambridge, and Quy : it seems probable that the mills which we know in the present day are built on the sites of the old mills and rely on the same water-power. The Survey goes into great detail : the mill at Pakenham in Suffolk is described as a winter mill,[2] because there was not water enough in the stream in summer to work it. But, with all the information that is given us, we are sometimes left at a loss. There was a mill at Balsham, but it could hardly have been a water-mill, I think, in that area, and no horses are enumerated as being available for it. Perhaps some of you who know the parish better than I do can solve the difficulty. The limits that are given us as to the divided ownership of some of the mills (*e. g.* at Sawston) and as to the manner in which the miller was remunerated by a commission, paid in kind, on the work actually done, whet the appetite for more information on this side of village economy.

[1] Jocelyn's *Chronicle* (Camden Society).
[2] *D. B.*, II. 361.

III

SELF-CENTRED GROUPS—MARKETS

In the last lecture I tried to contrast the Roman colonisation with the settlement of the English tribes, and to show how much the English held aloof from town life, and how little account they took of trade. The tradition of Roman civilisation survived throughout the country : in one city, Exeter, it seems to have maintained itself steadily through all the centuries of turmoil; and in every parish it is a problem as to how far Roman influence survived, or how soon it was revived.

To-day I wish to call your attention to the traces we find of the beginnings of trade. This was of two kinds : there came to be " populous places," which needed regular supplies of butter, eggs, and meat, and led to the beginning of *weekly markets ;* and there were also the occasional visits of traders from a distance, which eventually became organised in *fairs.* It is only about *markets* I shall speak to-day, that is, of trade among neighbours, reserving what I have to say about distant trade till next week.

When I speak of populous places, I do not mean such towns as we are familiar with in the present day, or even a village, but only a household which was so big, or so fully occupied, that it could not supply its own needs week by week, but made.a regular demand for produce. There were two different types of such households.

In the first place, there were forts or castles, in which soldiers were gathered to defend the realm, especially against the Danish raids. Warwick was built as a castle, containing the troops and munition-workers of the day.

There were, besides, abbeys, where the monks not only devoted themselves to maintaining and diffusing the Christian faith, but preserved ancient learning, and did their best for education and for organising industrial arts. Those who were engaged in the peaceful pursuit of the arts of life under the shadow of a monastery had to be catered for, and thus there was a demand for weekly supplies. Bury and Peter-borough were abbey towns which have grown into great importance. Many of the later abbeys were so well organised that they supplied their own needs, and never gave rise to a market; such were the great Yorkshire abbeys at Fountains and Rievaulx. There were, of course, military centres, like Win-chester and Shrewsbury, which have grown into large towns, but there is a great interest in the castle towns which have never grown up, but remain as mere fortresses with a market-place beside them. I do not know any of these in Cambridgeshire, but Castle Rising in Norfolk and Tattershall Castle in Lincolnshire are excellent examples.

In order to indicate the origin of weekly markets

and trade I have distinguished these different elements; but there were many towns where both these elements were combined, and the towns which grew most rapidly were both castle towns and abbey towns. After the Norman Conquest there was a great era of castle-building, and also of founding abbeys; the castle at Cambridge dates from William the Conqueror. Norwich has both a castle and an abbey, and both were founded in Norman times, and the *reason* of the origin of the town is a matter for conjecture; our knowledge only enables us to point out how some places of trade had their beginning, and why some places of trade grew and flourished.

Medieval towns were formed out of different elements, and an account of the way in which these elements were welded together in different cases involves a series of very long and intricate stories; all that is necessary for my immediate purpose is to point out that different forces were at work to bring about this result.

There was, in the first place, the compulsion of common authority and jurisdiction, which showed itself first in the authority of the owners of the land on which the town was built, and, eventually, in the responsibility of the citizens to collect taxes themselves and to enforce order themselves; there was also an element of coercion. We find traces, too, from very early times, of public spirit and desire to benefit the town, and this found expression in voluntary associations which provided for mutual help and benefits and were known as *gilds*.

The authority of the owners of the land was maintained in a great many cases, such as Manchester and Sheffield, till quite recent times (1833), but, as exercised in some of the abbey towns, this authority was very galling and much resented. At S. Albans the abbot insisted on the townsmen having their corn ground at the abbey mills and would not allow them to have hand-mills; this seems to us mere tyranny, but when the abbot had been at the expense of building and maintaining a mill, it must have been irritating if his tenants refused to make use of it. Similar causes of irritation arose in many places, notably at Norwich and Reading; and we may notice how many of the abbeys are protected from the townsmen by walls : that which is carried over the river at Bury is especially picturesque. There were very few inland towns which were protected by walls, whereas abbey walls are common enough, as at Hexham and Shaftesbury.

There are some words in common use which tell us of an old municipal revolution which took place in London in the twelfth century, when coercive authority in the town passed from the landowners to the inhabitants themselves. This change went on gradually, in one town after another, as charters conferred various privileges on the townsmen, and entrusted them with the duty of collecting taxes among themselves and the power of enforcing order and punishing crime. The rise of this new authority and power of civic self-government is often marked by the creation of a mayor. The first mention of a mayor of Cambridge is in 1235, and the earliest charter that is still preserved and may still be seen is that granted by King John in 1207.

Charters also granted the townsmen the permission to be associated together in gilds for mutual benefit. We all know how much dispute there has been in recent years about the " right to combine " in trades unions, and a charter often gave the townsmen a right to combine. The bodies which governed the town, and which acted from mutual convenience, often co-operated and took part in the same work : it has been a very frequent thing for the government of the town to be carried on in the hall of a gild.

To return now to market-places.

The position of the original market-place was probably fixed by the convenience of buyers in getting supplies, and of sellers in fetching them; and we cannot be surprised that, as the population changed its residence, or new roads were made, a change of the market-place was found convenient. The market-place at Peterborough was changed from the east end of the abbey to its present position at the west by Abbot Martin, about 1150; the town land, or empty space, was the original market in Norwich, and at Cambridge the market at the time of the Conquest was probably held near the present Castle Hill, in the pig-market or the hay-market. But sometimes we can see that the meeting-place of two roads has been a convenient position for the people who bought supplies : it was so at Carlisle, where there is a large triangular market, and an example of such a market-place has been preserved on the borders of our county in the little market-place at Fen Stanton.

There are no public buildings in Cambridge which remain to remind us of the life of the town—no old gild-hall, no prison ; but there is a gild-hall at Linton, where meetings could be held and goods could be stored ; and there is evidence of commercial activity at Swaffham Bulbeck.

We have, however, numberless examples of the sort of private houses in which the people lived. They were of two different types, the yard house and the corridor house. Both differed greatly from the houses we know in the residential quarters, say, of Kensington or of any modern town where the house fronts the street, and there is a little street or stable lane which gives access to the back-yard.

The essential feature in the medieval town houses was that there was access to the workshop, or yard, behind the house from the front. It is a very strange thing, but the Romans seem to have used these types of houses in some of the cities in this country,[1] and there is a tendency in the present day to abolish basements and revert to it, not only in villas, but in such rows of houses as Queen Anne Terrace. The yard house was commonly adopted for inns, of which there were a great many in Cambridge. The Falcon Yard was an admirable example of the old inn which had undergone very little alteration twenty years

[1] Haverfield, in the *Victoria County History* of Northamptonshire.

ago; and the old arrangements are still recognisable in the Lion Yard and the Blue Boar. The yard of the Rose has also been preserved for us in Rose Crescent.

The corridor houses had a passage that gave direct access to the back of the house, as well as a door to the front. We see passage houses all along Sidney Street and Trinity Street and all round the market-place. They were the common type of town house all over England through the Middle Ages, and when Englishmen began to settle in New England they built passage houses in the towns they planted there. Sometimes the passages were private, as they are here; but sometimes they were public thoroughfares, as they are in the rows of Great Yarmouth or the closes of Edinburgh.

At the close of the Middle Ages, in the time of Edward VI and Elizabeth, many market-shelters were built. The inconvenience of an open market, exposed to all sorts of weather, is a matter with which we are familiar in Cambridge. We often feel how hard it is on those who stand in the market, when one Saturday after another is wet; but what strikes us about these shelters, as about some of the oldest market-places, is that they were very small. Of course the women who came with baskets of butter and eggs could be packed very close, as we may see them in a French market-place, like that of Le Mans, or in the French part of Canada; but it is worth while to remember that the area from which supplies could be brought was very limited, and that the towns

27

could not extend indefinitely: they were limited by the supplies that were available. The old market cross at Cambridge has been swept away, though there is a picture of it, with a woman selling butter, in an edition of Foxe's *Martyrs*,[1] but there is a market shelter still remaining at Mildenhall.

The small scale on which provision is made is impressive, because it reminds us of an important fact which we are apt to overlook, namely, that the life of the towns in the Middle Ages was limited by the conditions of supply. Men could not draw very far afield for the food they needed; they could not draw very far afield for the materials on which they worked; they could not cater for distant purchasers. This means that they could not push their trade, as is done in modern times. The Londoners were anxious as to how it would be possible to feed all the people that crowded there, and they reckoned on selling English goods at places where they had the privilege of trading, and not by offering them cheap and by successful competition. These limitations affected the policy of the towns: each town aimed at making the most of its resources for the present and future benefit of the townsmen, rather than at growing to a great size. They were contented, in modern language, with few transactions and big profits on each sale, and thus some of the men who could take advantage of these conditions

---

[1] Edition of 1732. The woman is apparently selling yards of butter. Carter mentions butter as made up in yards, *Cambridgeshire*, p. 15.

became very rich. We look back on their regulations, and speak of the narrow spirit of monopoly which characterised them; and it is quite true that the towns were self-centred, but the townsmen were not specially selfish, as compared with townsmen to-day, for we have many monuments which show their public spirit and their anxiety to do something for the benefit of their own town in time to come. Of course the great example, in every village, of this public spirit is to be found in the parish church, but there are numberless benefactions of other kinds. There was the water supply, and conduit, which we feel to be distinctive, and for which we are indebted to Hobson the carrier; there were many charities for the support of those who were past work, like S. Eligius' almshouses; there were isolation hospitals, of which we are reminded by the Lepers' Chapel on the Newmarket Road, and, especially after the Reformation, there were schools, like the Perse School and the Green Coat School at Bottisham. Enthusiasm for the place where one lived and thrived may have been a very narrow sentiment, but it expressed itself in real public spirit.

IV

FAIRS AND DISTANT TRADE

THOUGH the English tribes did not take account of trade in their first settlements, and only gradually engaged in regular trade, it would be a mistake to suppose that the tradition of occasional trade at fairs, which were frequented by strangers from a distance, died out completely.

The great occasions of festival, with sacrifice and feasting, were opportunities for traffic which do not seem to have been neglected in heathen times in Ireland; and Gregory was anxious that some opportunities of festival should be found for the English convert at the newly-consecrated churches. He suggested that on the day of the nativity of the holy martyrs whose relics were deposited in any church the people " might build themselves huts from the boughs of trees," [1] and celebrate the solemnity with religious feasting. Five hundred years later we find that it was the custom of certain tenants of the Abbey of Durham to furnish booths for the feast of S. Cuthbert; and one is tempted to think of the stalls as distinguishing the trade which was carried on at fairs from the sale of produce which went on

[1] Bede, *Ecc. Hist.*, I. xxx. (A.D. 601).

at the weekly markets to which women came with their baskets.

There is very little mention of fairs before the Norman Conquest or in Domesday Book, but we hear a great deal of them in the Norman and Angevin reigns; and it is quite possible that some of them were held at the time of the Conquest, although there is no mention of them. But at all events it is clear that by far the greater part of the trade of the country, and especially of what we should call the foreign trade, was carried on at fairs through the Middle Ages and down to modern times. Aliens were not free to buy or sell in the chartered towns, but they could go to the fairs. They sold the products of other countries and manufactured goods of many sorts; and they expended the money they made in purchasing English wool and other raw materials for export.

Fairs, and the concourse of traders which they periodically brought about, led, in some cases, to the rise of a town. The site of Great Yarmouth was a mere sand-bank, but it was convenient for traffic, and the herring fair which was held there gave rise to the growth of a permanent population. There is another instance in our own neighbourhood, for it was the fair of S. Ives that led to the building of the town there; and the two fairs which are still held in Cambridge may at all events have been important elements in the growth of the town as a centre of trade. We hear of Midsummer Fair in the time of Henry III, and Stourbridge Fair maintained its importance in the eighteenth century. Defoe visited it, and has given a long description in his *Tour*, since he regarded it as the greatest fair in Europe, more important even than those at Frankfort and Leipzig.

" It is kept," he writes, " in a large Corn-field, near *Casterton*, extending from the Side of the River *Cam*, towards the Road, for about half a Mile Square.

" If the Husbandmen who rent the Land, do not get their Corn off before a certain Day in *August*, the Fair-Keepers may trample it under foot and spoil it to build their Booths, or Tents. . . . On the other Hand, to ballance that Severity, if the Fair-Keepers have not . . . clear'd the Field by another certain Day in *September*, the Plowmen may come in again, with Plow and Cart, and overthrow all . . . into the Dirt; and as for the Filth, Dung, Straw, &c. necessarily left by the Fair-Keepers, the Quantity of which is very great, it is the Farmers Fees, and makes them full amends for the trampling, riding, carting upon, and hardening the Ground.

" It is impossible to describe all the Parts and Circumstances of this Fair exactly; the Shops are placed in Rows like Streets, whereof one is call'd *Cheapside ;* and here, as in several other Streets, are all Sorts of Traders, who sell by Retale, and who come principally from *London*. . . . Goldsmiths, Toyshops, Brasiers, Turners, Milleners, Haberdashers, Hatters, Mercers, Drapers, Pewterers, China-Warehouses, and in a Word all Trades that can be named in *London ;* with Coffee-Houses, Taverns,

Brandy-Shops, and Eating-houses innumerable, and all in Tents, and Booths, as above.

" This great Street reaches from the Road, which, as I said goes from *Cambridge* to *New Market*, turning short out of it to the Right towards the River, and holds in a Line near half a Mile quite down to the River-side : In another Street parallel with the Road are like Rows of Booths, but larger, and more intermingled with Wholesale Dealers, and one Side, passing out of this last Street to the Left Hand, is a formal great Square, form'd of the largest Booths . . . which they call the *Duddery ;* whence the Name is deriv'd I could never yet learn. The Area of this Square is about 80 to a 100 Yards, where the Dealers have room before every Booth to take down, and open their Packs, and to bring in Waggons to load and unload.

" This Place is . . . peculiar to the Wholesale Dealers in the Woollen Manufacture. Here the Booths, or Tents are of a vast Extent, have different Apartments, and the Quantities of Goods they bring are so Great, that the Insides of them look like another *Blackwell Hall*, being as vast Ware-houses pil'd up with Goods to the Top. In this *Duddery*, as I have been inform'd, have been sold 100,000 Pounds worth of Woollen Manufactures in less than a Week's time ; besides the prodigious Trade carry'd on here, by Wholesale-men from *London*, and all Parts of *England*, who transact their Business wholly in their Pocket-Books, and meeting their Chapmen from all Parts, make up their Accounts, receive Money chiefly in

Bills, and take Orders: These they say exceed by far the Sales of Goods actually brought to the Fair, and deliver'd in Kind; it being frequent for the *London* Wholesale-men to carry back Orders from their Dealers for 10,000 Pounds worth of Goods a Man, and some much more. This especially respects those People, who deal in heavy Goods, as Wholesale Grocers, Salters, Brasiers, Iron-Merchants, Wine-Merchants, and the like; but does not exclude the Dealers in Woollen Manufactures, and especially in Mercery Goods of all sorts, the dealers in which generally manage their business in this manner.

" Here are Clothiers from *Hallifax, Leeds, Wakefield* and *Huthersfield*, in *Yorkshire*, and from *Rochdale, Bury*, &c., in *Lancashire*, with vast *Quantities* of *Yorkshire* Cloths, Kerseyes, Pennistons, Cottons, &c., with all sorts of *Manchester* Ware, Fustians, and things made of Cotton Wool; of which the Quantity is so great, that they told me there were near 1000 Horse-Packs of such Goods from that side of the Country, and these took up a side and half of the *Duddery* at least; also a Part of a Street of Booths were taken up with Upholsterers' Ware, such as Tickings, Sackings, *Kidderminster* Stuffs, Blankets, Rugs, Quilts, &c.

" In the *Duddery* I saw one Ware-house, or Booth with six Apartments in it, all belonging to a Dealer in *Norwich* Stuffs only, and who they said had there above 20,000 Pounds Value in those Goods, and no other.

"Western Goods had their Share here also, and several Booths were filled as full with Serges, Du-Roys, Druggets, Shalloons, Cantaloons, *Devonshire* Kersies, &c., from *Exeter*, *Taunton*, *Bristol*, and other Parts West, and some from *London* also.

"But all this is still out done, at least in show, by two Articles, which are the peculiars of this Fair, and do not begin till the other Part of the Fair, *that is to say for the Woollen Manufacture* begins to draw to a Close: These are the WOOLL, and the HOPS, as for the Hops, there is scarce any Price fix'd for Hops in *England*, till they know how they sell at *Sturbridge* Fair; the Quantity that appears in the Fair is indeed prodigious, and they, *as it were*, possess a large Part of the Field on which the Fair is kept, to themselves; they are brought directly from *Chelmsford* in *Essex*, from *Canterbury* and *Maidstone* in *Kent*, and from *Farnham* in *Surrey*, besides what are brought from *London*, the Growth of those and other Places." [1]

The volume of trade done at Stourbridge Fair in the eighteenth century was still very great; it was a vast concourse, and there is a map which shows its extent and the parts of it where different classes of goods were sold. We hear, too, from Blomefield that the Lepers' Chapel was used as a repository for the stuff to build the Fair,[2] and it is spoken of again by Carter in 1819, with special reference to the extreme discomfort of the crowd of people who

[1] Defoe, *Tour* (1724) I. 122–125.
[2] Blomefield, *Collectanea Cantabrigiensia* (1750) p. 171.

slept in the booths.[1] But long before that time fairs
had, generally speaking, declined in importance, and
business was done regularly in shops where stocks
were kept all the year round. It was at the time
of the Crusades that the fairs had their greatest
importance, as opportunities of trade, relatively to
the total trade of the country. Bishop Grosseteste of
Lincoln [2] wrote to the Countess advising her as to
the different fairs at which it was best worth while
to replenish the stock of goods of different sorts which
she needed for her household.

The Crusades were a great military and missionary
movement, and the intercourse between the near
East and the West to which they gave rise, as well
as between the northern realms and the Mediter-
ranean, had an extraordinary influence in promoting
the trade and national progress of many parts of
Europe. The rise of Venice and Genoa is a mark of
this side of the Crusades; but it is our business
to-day to notice the signs which remain of the share
which Cambridgeshire had in this activity.

The Knights Templars devoted themselves to the
missionary and military side of the crusading struggle.
They were a great international military order; and
we know that they had great importance in Cambridgeshire. The Round Church is a monument of
their enthusiasm for the undertaking which General
Allenby has accomplished in our day, and for rescuing

[1] Carter, *Cambridgeshire*, p. 29.
[2] The Rules of S. Robert, printed in Walter of Henley's
Husbandry (ed. 1890).

from domination by the infidel the places which seem specially sacred to all Christian men. The Round Church is not our only memorial of the Military Orders, for the Templars had a preceptory at Great Wilbraham, and the Hospitallers at Shingay were large proprietors; but nothing remains there except foundations, which tell us little or nothing.

The commercial activity of the time took shape in the founding of new towns and the expansion of old ones. King Edward I did a great deal in founding new towns, both in his possessions in the south of France and in his realm at home. He had a keen eye for a site which offered facilities for commerce. King's Lynn and Kingston-upon-Hull were among the cities he created, and he was not very scrupulous about respecting the claims of other proprietors, and refraining from injurious competition. A similar policy had been followed by some great ecclesiastics. Bishop Poore of Salisbury moved his church and the city, with its inhabitants, from Old Sarum to the present site, where the water supply was more ample, and Bishop Robert obtained a charter from king David to erect a burgh at St. Andrews, and invited burgesses from Berwick-upon-Tweed to settle there and administer its affairs.

When there was so much activity in laying out new towns or suburbs, we cannot be surprised that a great deal of attention was given to town-planning. The best examples of this are to be found in some of the towns in the south of France, such as Montpazier and Carcassonne, but it is at least arguable that the bishops had similar plans in mind, though they adapted them to local circumstances, when they laid out St. Andrews and Salisbury. The desire to imitate these foreign cities is very clearly seen in some of the public buildings of the later Middle Ages, especially in the town hall of Much Wenlock; but, as I know of no Cambridgeshire instances which still survive, I shall not attempt to follow out this line of study.

In the Eastern counties, however, we find great alterations of the ground-plan of the town which are, at any rate, a local commemoration of this great period of commercial development.

The Roman town of Cambridge had been on the north side of the river, on the slope from S. Giles' Church to the Huntingdon Road; and Freeman thinks that the resuscitated English town had hardly extended beyond those limits. William the Conqueror had pulled down a great many houses, however, and it seems probable that the inhabitants found new homes on the south side of the river along Bridge Street. The settlement of Jews, which generally was established on the outskirts of the town, would lead us to suppose that in the time of Henry I the town did not extend southward beyond the Divinity Schools and the old site of All Saints' Church; but we fortunately possess a very complete account of the town in the time of Edward I,[1] and we see that it then covered the area marked by Mill Lane, Pembroke Street, Corn Exchange Street, and

---

[1] *Rotuli Hundredorum*, I.

Hobson Street.   There was thus a great extension in area, and we see what great facilities were given for merchants, in the numerous inns of Petty Cury and the market-place.

The market-place itself is a memento of the provision which was made for business; the men of the time were not satisfied to provide for the market women who brought weekly supplies, but laid out a large market in which stalls could be erected, similar to those which were provided at fairs, and where the stocks of goods could be displayed.

The stalls were usually arranged in rows, as we see them at present; they were movable, and put up only for the market-day; but it came to be convenient to erect more permanent stalls, especially for the shambles, or butchers' shops.

We find evidence in many cities of a great deal of encroachment by permanent stalls and houses on what had been the open area of the market-place as originally laid out.   We can trace the original area of the market-place in Cambridge by noting the corridor houses which surround it.   They run along Peas Hill and Wheeler Street and Guildhall Place, as well as on the east and north sides of the market-place itself.   The town hall would be likely to stand within the square, as it does at present, and the shops which are grouped round it must be regarded as encroachments on the original open site.   The still more serious encroachments which are represented in coloured engravings of the market-place, were destroyed by the great fire in 1849.   When you

39

have occasion to visit other towns, and see other old market-places, it is quite worth while to try and notice how far there has been encroachment on an open place.

The reigns of Edward I and Edward II and the first half of Edward III's were the great period of medieval prosperity. Till this time the country, as a whole, had been making material progress, and during the twelfth and thirteenth centuries this progress had been generally rapid. There is evidence to show that Cambridgeshire shared in this prosperity; for, besides the wealth that was needed to provide for immediate wants, there was plenty to spare which could be used in beautiful buildings, and this has been preserved in our churches. The nuns of S. Radegund were able to build their Chapter House, and we see its remains in the cloisters of Jesus College; the churches of Little S. Mary's, S. Edward's, and S. Michael's parishes were also built at this time. All these came to be used partly as college chapels, and Hervey of Stanton, whose benefaction has been absorbed in Trinity College, was also busied in providing S. Michael's Church. There was similar activity in several country parishes, at Over and Shepreth and Bottisham. But with the middle of the fourteenth century this steady progress came suddenly to an end. There was a dreadful pestilence, called the Black Death, which swept over Europe and carried off about half of the population in town and country. We have a wonderfully graphic account of the circumstances which brought the infection in a cargo of Eastern goods to Genoa, and we can trace the terrible desolation, and the horror it caused, as it gradually spread over Europe. There is local evidence that Cambridge suffered as acutely as other places. The survivors did not need as many parish churches; S. Giles' was united with All Saints' in Castro, and with S. Peter's. Proposals were mooted for the union of S. Michael's with S. Mary's the Great, or with All Saints' in Jewry, as the present parish of All Saints' was then known; and the burial-ground, where the dead were interred, has never been built upon; it still stands as a vacant space opposite the County Court, close to the Huntingdon Road.

These relics of the Black Death help us to remember that Cambridge was not spared. We have no statistics, as chroniclers attempted to give for some other towns, but we have contemporary records that show the effects of the plague in country places as well as in towns. There is an interesting inscription in the tower of the church at Ashwell, though it is not easy to decipher.

There is also evidence of the great scarcity of labour and the desolation from which there seemed to be no hope of recovery. We read a most mournful account of Chesterton, but perhaps the most graphic and detailed statement comes from Bottisham.

How much the cost of living had increased is shown by the fact that a religious foundation which had been made in 1348, proved to be quite inadequate in 1351, and the whole had to be re-founded.

The difficulty of carrying through any great

41

undertaking may be borne in on our minds by the length of time which was required for the completing of Great S. Mary's. It was begun in 1478. As Fuller says, " all church work is slow, but the mention of S. Mary's mindeth me of church work indeed, so long was it from the foundation to the finishing thereof." The University gave great assistance in collecting funds; but, though the old church had been burnt down in 1290, it was not till 1478 that the foundations were laid, and the new church attempted, and the tower was not finished till 1608. You can still see in the west porch the inscription to John Warren, the master mason, who " with the tower his own life finished."

V

ROYAL CONTROL

THE Black Death marked the beginning of a long period of decadence; and, when recovery began, it was largely due to the strong monarchy of the Tudors and the manner in which they exercised control over many localities that had hitherto pursued an independent, or, at least, a self-centred life of their own. I make this statement very confidently, though I am well aware that it is very difficult to get any standard by which to measure changes in national prosperity; indeed, from some points of view it might seem that the working-classes were particularly well off in the fifteenth century.

It is also true that the cloth trade was flourishing in many parts of England, and was being diffused in villages and not confined to corporate towns; there was great prosperity among growers of wool, but Cambridgeshire had little part in this development. For some reason while Suffolk was "full of manufacturers," these were never in Cambridgeshire, and therefore this exceptional prosperity does not concern us. In our county there was a shortage of labour, and it was necessary for employers to pay very high wages to get any work done; but even

43

this did not benefit the working-classes in the long run, for many people changed their habits and did not give as much employment as they had done before the pestilence, while all other classes suffered severely. The Government could not collect the taxes which were formerly paid, and many towns which had been flourishing continued in a ruinous condition for years and years. But it is of a change in the habits of the great landed proprietors that I especially wish to speak.

In the prosperous times it had been the habit of many proprietors to have their estates cultivated, and to move from one estate to another, so as to eat up the produce of each estate in turn, rather than to collect all the food at one centre; thus each of the great magnates was frequently on the move, with his retinue, from one castle to another. These castles were very bare, and it seems to have been the fashion to take the wall-hangings and such-like furnishings from one bare house to another, so that there was an enormous retinue of household retainers to carry out the removals. The landowners were interested in seeing that each estate was well culti-vated, so that they should have plentiful supplies on each estate. At the zenith of medieval prosperity the art of agriculture was carried on effectively. Though we do not think of the medieval baron as keenly interested in his estate or, as Lord Ernle says,[1] visiting markets and " fumbling in the recesses of his armour for samples of corn," still, the lords of

[1] *English Farming.*

44

Berkeley, in Gloucestershire, were men who interested themselves personally in estate management for generations. It is remarkable, too, that the Manual of estate management which the steward of Christchurch at Canterbury wrote at the end of the reign of Henry III, continued to hold its own for centuries; it had a wide circulation, and there are many copies in existence, but there was no fresh experience which enabled any one to supersede it till the time of Henry VIII.

But after the Black Death, when there was so much difficulty in getting labour, the proprietors had no longer any interest, so far as we can see, in encouraging cultivation. They could get the best income by dispensing with labour as much as possible, and using their land for feeding sheep, thus getting an income by the sale of wool. In this way they got larger returns with less trouble; and there is ample evidence, both in the statute-book and in literature, of the turning of arable land into pasturage, but the putting down of ploughs and the discontinuance of employment were generally looked upon as a social evil and a political danger. The policy of the Crown was quite clear; there was a constant endeavour to make the landed gentry settle on their estates as resident proprietors, and to take an active part in enforcing law and order throughout the country.

The Government had to face many difficulties in trying to carry out this scheme, and the struggle went on for about a century and a half; but at last the new policy was successful, and under James I

45

and Charles I the temptation to take to sheep-farming had ceased to be strongly felt, and the landed gentry were more inclined to settle on their estates; men who had made money as merchants were also inclined to buy property in land and turn it to the best account.

There is a great difference between the houses which the magnates had built in the old time of prosperity and the houses of the landed gentry in Tudor and Stuart times. The magnates had built castles, defensible, but very uncomfortable, which were large enough to house a retinue. The chief feature in the castle was the hall, a huge living-room where the retinue ate and slept, and where existence must have been very squalid. Even the humbler manor houses were laid out on the same principle, with a great living-room for the household. The country gentry of the Tudor and Stuart times, on the other hand, built beautiful houses, which had little in the way of defences, and surrounded themselves with pictures and treasures.

In Cambridgeshire we have very little trace of the magnates who occupied one house after another in turn; though the de Veres were possibly only temporary visitors at Castle Camps. The only great proprietor who seems to have been much on the move was the bishop. He had a castle at Wisbech, and a residence at Downham in the Isle, as well as at Balsham.

There is, however, in Pythagoras Hall, a remarkable and almost unique example of the thirteenth-century manor house, and there are other houses which tell of proprietors who ceased to employ their tenants in agriculture and preferred to use their land for pasture-farming and for game. At Childerley, Sir John Cutts got rid of all his tenantry and built a beautiful mansion with a garden in front of it, and something very similar was done at Landwade; in the Tudor times the royal policy, which Bishop Morton helped to carry out, had been very successful, and the great households and retinues had been broken up. Those who wished to dwell in safety could not attempt to keep a retinue of men-at-arms, but had to rely on physical features, or strong walls, such as we see at Madingley, or more commonly on the moats which can be much more easily made in a country where there is little building material. The moats became common in the fifteenth century, and are of great importance in the defences of Tattershall Castle; and there are many examples round the manor houses and farm buildings in this county and in Suffolk. There are doubtless many which I do not know, but I have seen moats at Borough Green, at Sawston, at East Hatley, and at Croydon; and they must have been effective defences, not so much against soldiers, as against riots and disorderly neighbours.

The old country magnates had been men of great wealth who were practically independent of the Crown; the new landed gentry were proud of being county magistrates, and of exercising the responsibilities which the Crown conferred upon them, and the houses

47

which were put up in the seventeenth century and onwards, such as Wimpole, or Hatley S. George, and Horseheath, Gog-ma-gogs, now pulled down, but fully described in Defoe's *Tour*, were quite without defences.

The recovery of the realm, which began under the Tudors, was, in part, the consequence of the great increase which took place in royal control. I have already pointed out how important the cohesive forces had been in regard to the towns, and under the Tudors it was a cohesive force which treated the realm as a whole, and did not allow local interests or class interests to assert themselves. It might have come about in some other way, but as a matter of fact it was by the exercise of personal authority by the monarch and his council that the realm was, as it were, pulled together, and made conscious of itself as a whole, and of its duty to the king and the community.

It was thus much more possible to devise a national policy in regard to the life of the country : in the Middle Ages each city determined its own policy, but now they were encouraged to co-operate with one another. Citizens began to think more of the defence of the realm, and not of their own district, of the food supply of the realm and the possibilities of increasing it, and of the trade of the realm and the possibilities of pushing it and opening up further progress. So long as each part was self-centred, its progress was limited by its resources; but when the resources of the whole realm were taken into account,

48

and it was seen that England had plenty of corn to export, and plenty of wool to work up as materials, there was no longer anxiety about growing too fast. The new policy of the Crown was that of pushing trade in all directions, and of trying to make sure that the trade was so controlled as to react favourably on the prosperity of the country as a whole, both in peace and war. This policy, which was carefully thought out and systematically pursued by Lord Burleigh, is generally known as the mercantile system, so far as its external aspects are concerned; the aim was that England as a whole should hold its own with other nations in Europe. But in an inland county like Cambridgeshire we have very little to do with the external aspects. Cambridgeshire had no part, like Devonshire, in the voyages of discovery, nor, like the seamen of the East coast, in carrying on the fishing business : it had little direct part in the work of colonisation, though Harvard's friends paid him the compliment of calling the town where his University was founded after the English University of which he had been a member. Bunker's Hill may also have borrowed its name.

But we want to look chiefly at the internal life of the country. To an extent which never occurred before it was treated as a whole, and there were regulations of all sorts, not by local authority, but by royal proclamations or parliamentary enactments, and there was a possibility of much more division of labour, and of each part of the country specialising

E   49

in what it could do best. The increase of royal
regulation and control went on from the Tudor times
till the Civil War, and the specialisation of Cambridgeshire in agriculture and the improvement of agriculture went on all through the eighteenth century;
we can still point to some monuments of both
tendencies.

We have had some experience lately of attempts
to organise the resources of the realm in a great
emergency, and to direct skill and labour to carrying
on a war for the defence of the realm as a whole.
In Elizabethan England an effort was made to
organise the realm as a regular thing, so as to foster
the future prosperity of the whole, and make each
part contribute to the common good. There was an
elaborate machinery for fixing the rates of wages,
and for securing a sufficient supply of agricultural
labour.

There was also a very elaborate machinery for
regulating the market and for seeing that the food
supply was used so as to last all the year round,
and that it was, as far as possible, rendered available
for all districts. Officials, called clerks of the market,
were charged with this delicate duty; they had
originally been concerned as purveyors in getting
supplies for the royal household, but in Tudor times
they came to have a supervision over transactions in
all sorts of goods. The special arrangements which
were made for the poor in years of scarcity, by selling
them corn at a reduced price, paved the way for the
introduction of a system of Poor Relief. The magis-

trates and clerks of the market had to apply the general instructions of the royal council, and to see that the interest of the consumer, who wished to have corn cheap, and the encouragement of the producer, so that he might go on cultivating, were both taken into account. It is noticeable that in England, as compared with most continental countries, there was a tendency to encourage the producers of corn to furnish a large supply and maintain the profit of the plough. We are reminded of the minute care of a paternal government at this time by the bells which were provided to manage the conduct of business in a well-ordered market.[1] The medieval towns did not have bells of their own which could summon the citizens suddenly; they were often content to bargain for the use of the church bells, as was done here and in Ipswich.[2] But after Elizabeth's time market bells became common, and bell turrets are noticeable in many towns, like S. Ives, where markets were held. The regulations with regard to fire hooks are another instance of the minuteness of royal supervision.

One result of this general system of regulation was that each district was better able to devote itself to the activities for which it was most fitted. This comes out in the history of towns, but it is also clear in the counties. Some places were

[1] On the 1st of March [1566] the Vice-Chancellor decreed that the Taxors' servants should, every Saturday after one o'clock, take care that the Market Bell be rung (Cooper's *Annals*, v. 299).

[2] Wodderspoon, *Memorials of Ipswich.*

encouraged to devote themselves to the fishing trades;
as new land was brought into cultivation, some of
the light soils began to be used for the sheep-farming
for which they were adapted, but Cambridgeshire,
on the whole, was devoted to tillage and cattle-
rearing.

These were prosecuted with vigour. The increased
facilities for marketing corn gave farmers the
opportunity to alter their practice. Many of them
had been accustomed to grow corn for their own
subsistence and live on the produce of their land,
and it was a great change when they took to farming
for the market, and selling the produce they secured.
Farming became a trade, like other trades, in which
the energetic man could make money; it was not
merely an occupation by which a certain number of
people lived. There was an extraordinary impulse
to agriculture when this new aim to push the business and increase the production began to be generally
operative.

Great pains were taken during this period to extend
the area which was cultivated; marshes were re-
claimed from the sea, and here in Cambridgeshire
great schemes were undertaken for saving the country
from inundations and flooding by the rivers. The
improvement of traffic and prevention of flood were
the two objects which Bishop Morton seems to have
had in mind, and the Bedford rivers are constant
reminders of the success which at length attended
the scheme and turned the Isle of Ely from being
wild country into a great stretch of rich arable land.

There was also a change of agricultural method which was of first-rate importance : this was the introduction of convertible husbandry, by which the fields, instead of being permanently used for tillage or as commons for feeding cattle, were alternately used for grazing and for growing corn. This was an immense improvement on the old three-field system. For some reason it had been very generally adopted in other counties before it was taken up in Cambridgeshire; it did not become general here till the end of the eighteenth and beginning of the nineteenth centuries. This agricultural revolution is very difficult to follow, as it went on for centuries in different counties, and a further difficulty arises from the fact that it has been commonly spoken of as " enclosing," and confused with the movement for increased sheepfarming, from which it was quite distinct. In Cambridgeshire, partly because it was so late, we have extraordinarily careful discussions of the good and evil of the change by very competent men at the time it occurred. There were two directions in which a great saving was effected by the new system : it was far better to feed the cattle in separate closes, where they could be properly attended to, than to let them wander together on the common waste, where there was more risk of infection. The land of the common waste was not made the most of when it was not improved, either for tillage or pasture, but left in its primitive condition. It was also of great importance to be set free from the tyranny of routine, and forced to follow the same custom

53

as other neighbours, instead of being free to do the best one could for the land. The advocates of the new system of convertible husbandry were certainly over-sanguine about the results to be expected,[1] and they pushed on the change in some places in a ruthless manner which showed that they were heedless of their poor neighbours. But it can hardly be doubted that the change was a real improvement in the country as a whole, and the advantages at length approved themselves in Cambridgeshire, as they had done in other parts of the country. It is also true that the old-fashioned system, when carefully attended to, held its own in certain parishes. The great herd of milch-kine fed together on the fen at Cottenham, and the owners of common rights appointed order-makers [2] who administered affairs so that they were able to make good account of the common use of the common waste.

[1] Fitzherbert, *Surveyinge.*
[2] *Camden Miscellany*, XII.

VI

FOOTPRINTS

IN this last lecture I hope to give you a short summary of the main points to which I have directed your attention throughout the course. I have been directing your attention to what are, in Longfellow's phrase, " footprints in the sands of time." We may, perhaps, change the figure and think of the church in every parish as a monument which has stood for many ages, and note how different generations have left their marks upon it.

There is something in the cathedral of Ely to remind us of each generation for centuries. There is the great Norman nave, built of stone which came across the seas from Caen. It was begun about 1083 and finished in 1130, just about the time of Domesday Book, and the Galilee about the time of Magna Carta. The extreme east end of the choir, with its pointed windows, dates from the time of Henry III, and was built by Hugh of Northwold, Bishop of Ely 1229–1254. Then the disaster which had long threatened the monks overtook the church: the great central tower fell on February 22, 1322, and broke down the three western bays of the choir in its ruin. But the sacrist, Alan of Walsingham, who was a great architectural genius, set about repairing the disaster at once, and finished the Lantern, which is the characteristic feature of Ely cathedral, in 1342. This feature seems to have given rise to conscious imitation in the towers of the parish churches at Sutton and Cheveley.

The restoration of the ruined portion of the choir was begun in 1332 by Bishop Hotham, who left money for carrying on the work; and in spite of the labour difficulties which the Black Death caused, it was completed in 1361. It serves as an excellent example of the beautiful decorative work which was characteristic of the early period of Edward III. There are also chapels and windows of the fifteenth century, which give opportunity for a greater display of glass than was provided for in earlier times; and so we have in this one building outward and visible marks of every stage of the building art from the Conquest to the Reformation.

The work of church-building went on not only in the cathedral church, but in every parish as well. Very often one age has wished to build something new-fashioned, and has destroyed the work of previous generations. In the fifteenth century, when the rich clothiers had much money at their disposal, the love of colour was more fashionable than it had been before, and the men of the time were particularly ruthless in knocking large windows into the old walls; they were fond, too, of adding towers which could carry a peal of bells. But there are a great many parish churches in which we can readily detect these later

56

alterations and form some idea of the original structure. We have no wooden churches, such as were commonly built in the times before the Conquest; but S. Bene't's, at Cambridge, which had been a wooden church, was burned by the Danes in A.D. 1010, and the tower, which was built of stone after that event, has the " long and short work " which was a sort of attempt to reproduce in stone the appearance of a timbered building. Without making invidious selections, we can see how many periods of architecture are represented in the parishes just round Cambridge: there is a characteristic Norman church at Coton; an early English church at Cherry Hinton; decorated churches at Trumpington and Fulbourne, and a perpendicular church at Great Shelford.

In many cases a mere fragment remains to testify to the original character of a stone which has been repaired or rebuilt out of all knowledge. A great many churches have some fragment of Norman work which shows what a wonderful time of architectural activity there was in the reigns after the Conquest; thus, for example, we can pick out the original chancel arch of Picot's church in S. Giles', Cambridge.

It is often interesting to trace the ground plan of a church and see how it has been added to, bit by bit. The normal course of change in this respect has been worked out in Wakefield Church by the late Mr. Micklethwaite. It is not hard to find in almost every parish church object-lessons which give children a sense of connection with some period in the past. I remember spending one hour between trains in

57

looking at a church in Ashbourne, in Derbyshire, and being delighted to find that a mistress had taken a class of children there to illustrate something that came into their lesson from the parish church.

This is not only possible in regard to the fabric of the church, but also in regard to the decorations and furniture of the church. The woodwork at King's College Chapel, with the true lovers' knot in which the initials of Henricus Rex and Anna Regina are intertwined, tells us of the brief period when this description was possible, and the beautiful screen and rood-loft at Guilden Morden, and another, as well as stalls, at Balsham, illustrate the munificence of the gilds, who were associated with the parish clergy in serving the church. Cambridgeshire is not so rich in beautiful screens as some other counties, such as Norfolk or Devonshire, and the account which William Dowsing gives of his deliberate work of destruction is painful reading. He was a conscientious man, with a misplaced sense of duty, and he did his work very thoroughly. There has also been a very general loss of the mural paintings, of which mere traces can be seen in many churches, but this may have been due to such influences as climate, rather than to deliberate destruction. The most striking picture that remains is the S. Christopher at Impington.

There are, however, many personal memorials which help to record the history of the county; such as the brasses which commemorate the knights and great magnates of the thirteenth century at

Trumpington, and at Westley Waterless, and two magnificent brasses in the chancel at Balsham.

Only a few fragments of ancient glass have been left for the most part; but there is a wonderfully interesting heraldic window at Wimpole, which gives the family tree of William de Ufford, 2nd Earl of Suffolk, who heard of the revolt of the men of Norfolk, and went disguised as a squire to warn Richard II of that dangerous rising.

There are numerous monuments which tell of the families which settled as residents in the county. Many of these have since left. There were the Cottons at Landwade [1] and Madingley, of whom the most distinguished member built the house at Hatley S. George; the Darrells at Shudy Camps; the Hardwicks at Wimpole; the Manners at Cheveley; and the Stewarts at Teversham.[2]

There is also a good deal of church plate that is not only of interest, but of value. During the Reformation period there had been a very general looting of church plate by the extremists in the Government. They made an exception in 1552 by directing the Commissioners to leave in each parish one " cup " for the communion of the laity.[3] It was not till 1567 that systematic attempts were made to replace the mischief done by these ravages. Careful inquiries were made by Archbishop Parker, and the

[1] Thomas Cotton was Sheriff of Cambridgeshire in 1287, Carter, *Cambridgeshire*, p. 230.
[2] Blomefield, p. 185.
[3] Bloxham, *Principles of Gothic Architecture* (1882), III, 184.

churchwardens were induced to provide a number of "cups," which were made by Fish of Norwich, and apparently cost £5 apiece,[1] so that by this exercise of ecclesiastical authority, chalices, with the name of the parish upon them, were provided in a very large number of parishes in the archdeaconry.

They are seen to be more common in Cambridgeshire than in other counties, and we may feel in such a case as this that they were probably due to the special efforts of Bishop Coxe or some other ecclesiastic, and did not come haphazard. The special characteristics of a county may perhaps be ultimately traced in large measure to the tastes and aims of the people in the county.

The presence of the University and the Colleges was doubtless a great influence in the history of Cambridgeshire. I am inclined to suspect that the position held by the University as Clerk of the Market [2] or the Act which required College rents to be paid in corn, and not in money, may have had some influence in delaying the agricultural revolution in Cambridgeshire. It is possible, however, that this is accounted for on purely agricultural grounds: here and there in Cambridgeshire there were excellent arrangements for carrying on the use of the common waste to good purpose, and there may have been no general desire to get rid of the wastes and substitute separate closes for pasturing the cattle.

---

[1] Churchwardens' Accounts, Great St. Mary's.
[2] The University powers as Clerk of the Market were a great grievance (Cooper, *Annals*, v. 47, 57, 187).

There certainly were resident gentry who took an active part in the work of agricultural improvement : Sir Roger Jenyns of Bottisham, who was much interested in the welfare of the parish and founded Bottisham School,[1] and the experiments in irrigation which were made at Babraham by Pallavicino [2] showed that the present Lord Lieutenant was not the first of the landowners there to realise the importance of doing his best for agriculture. Vancouver and Gooch, in their Reports on the Agriculture of Cambridge, call attention to the intelligent interest taken by the representative of the Bendyshes at Barrington, by Mr. Hurrel at Foxton, and by Mr. Hicks at Wilbraham.

Similar influences were doubtless at work in securing for Cambridgeshire a share in the great improvement of facilities for traffic by wheeled vehicles which occurred in the eighteenth century. Cambridge had been well provided with primitive roads and Roman roads, and local roads had gradually acquired importance in the Middle Ages; but the draining of the fens rendered it possible to revert to a disused line of traffic, and an Act of Parliament was procured in the eighteenth century for making the direct road from Cambridge to Ely by Streatham, instead of continuing to go round by Ald. Steps to improve the town as regards traffic were also taken in 1788.[3]

The history of Cambridgeshire opens up a vista

[1] E. Hailstone, *History of Bottisham* (Camb. Antiq. Soc.), p. 42.
[2] Arthur Young, *Annals*, v. 16, p. 177, quoted by Gooch, *Agriculture of Cambridgeshire*, 1811, p. 258.
[3] 28 George III. c. 64.

of indefinite extent, if we start from familiar objects, and ask the right questions about them and try to find the answers; and we shall find that this humble method of inquiry about familiar things enables us to extend our knowledge of other parts of England. Probably few of us are native, of Cambridgeshire; we all have associations and interests with some other county as well. I was brought up in Dumfriesshire, and through the Earls of Huntingdon there are curious links of connection between that distant border county and the fen country. But we shall make most speed if we are content to compare our own county with some of its neighbours : the contrasts as well as the resemblances between Cambridge and Suffolk are very interesting. Cambridgeshire, like Suffolk, had a paucity of good building-stone : but Cambridgeshire was enabled by its waterways to fetch Northamptonshire stone from a distance, while Suffolk made the most of the flints which were available within its own borders. Cambridgeshire had a great abbey at Ely, as Suffolk had at Bury, and the history of these great rivals and of their influence on their neighbours gives us a vivid picture of what abbeys were, and of the parts they took in the life of England. But there are contrasts too; the histories of the two counties supplement one another. Cambridgeshire was cut off from the sea, while Suffolk had an important port at Ipswich, and is full of monuments which remind us of its overseas trade. Cambridgeshire was purely agricultural, and a centre of internal trade, while Suffolk was full of manufactures; the fifteenth century, which was one of decadence in Cambridgeshire, was the time of the prosperity of the Suffolk clothiers. The migration of manufactures to Yorkshire and the west of England caused terrible unemployment in Suffolk, with which the magistrates tried to deal by introducing new industries, but this difficulty could not have been felt in Cambridgeshire at all. The strangers who came to Kersey, and other villages in Suffolk, were probably attracted by the facilities for getting wool to weave; the strangers who came to Cambridgeshire were brought to dig and drain, as they did at Thorney. There is a parallelism, but there is plenty of contrast between counties that are close neighbours, and when we institute comparisons with other parts of England we find that Cambridgeshire had little need for defence, while Cheshire and Shropshire, like Northumberland and Cumberland, were border counties, where the differences of two races, or the rivalries of two realms, long continued to be causes of disturbance.

But I venture to plead that by studying the traces which remain of its own history in each county we have the best prospect of rendering the history of England vivid and real to ourselves, and to those whom we teach.

Printed in the United States
By Bookmasters